LEARNING
TALMUD

LEARNING
TALMUD

A Guide
to
Talmud Terminology
and
Rashi
Commentary

SCOT A. BERMAN

JASON ARONSON INC.
Northvale, New Jersey
Jerusalem

Design by Pamela Roth.

This book was set in 11 point ITC Garamond by A-R Editions, Madison, WI.

Library of Congress Cataloging-in-Publication Data
Berman, Scot A.
    Learning Talmud : a guide to Talmud terminology and Rashi commentary / Scot A.
Berman.
        p.   cm.
    ISBN 0-7657-5958-6 (alk. paper)
    1. Talmud—Terminology. 2. Aramaic language—Glossaries, vocabularies, etc.
3. Rashi, 1040-1105—Language—Glossaries, etc. I. Title.
    BM503.6.B47 1997
    296. 1'2'0014—dc21   96-39697

Manufactured in the United States of America. Jason Aronson Inc. offers books and
cassettes. For information and catalog write to Jason Aronson Inc., 230 Livingston
Street, Northvale, NJ 07647.

This book is dedicated
in memory of
my father

שמעון יעקב בן הלל פסח ז״ל

Sterling J. Berman

CONTENTS

Preface   ix

Introduction   xiii

PART I   TALMUD TERMS   1

Using the Glossary   3
To the Student   5
To the Teacher   7
Glossary of Terms   9

PART II   RASHI COMMENTARY   53

Section 1—Aspects of Rashi Commentary   58
   Rashi on Mishna   58
   Rashi on Talmud   61
     General Aspects   61
     Aspects of Explaining מִדְרְשֵׁי הֲלָכָה   65
     Language Aspects   66

Section 2—Common Rashi Words and Phrases   69

PREFACE

The study of Talmud has been the preoccupation of the Jewish people since it was first redacted. In truth, the Talmud itself is an outgrowth of hundreds of years of an evolving Oral Tradition.

As a teacher of Talmud for many years, I have been fascinated by the Talmud's structure and the ways of its commentators. I am constantly searching for emerging patterns that might make it easier for my students to comprehend the text.

This book represents the outcome of that search. It is divided into two parts. Part I is a glossary of Talmud terms. The glossary is not a list of common words or general rules but rather a listing of words that go beyond their literal meaning and perform a specific function in the Talmud. (See introduction for elaboration.) Part II is a reference guide for the use of Rashi commentary on Talmud. Section 1 of Part II surveys Rashi's method of Talmud commentary. Section 2 contains a list of common Rashi words and phrases.

With so many good English guides to Talmud study already available, I believe it is necessary to justify the need for yet another.

While several handbooks deal with words and their meanings, few engage in how these words operate precisely in the context of the Talmud. The purpose and contribution of the Talmud Terms Glossary in Part I is that it explains how the Talmud uses its language. The guide to Rashi's commentary on Talmud in Part II is the first of its kind in English. It should be of great value to both the beginning student and the more advanced student in becoming familiar with what Rashi is trying to accomplish in his commentary and the language he uses.

Many people have been involved in contributing to the completion of this work. Rabbi Tsvi Blanchard, former principal of the Ida Crown Jewish Academy and founder of the "Mesivta" Talmud Program, provided the theoretical framework and forum that allowed me to develop this work. I would like to thank, collectively. all the Rabbanim associated with the "Mesivta" who offered keen insight into teaching Talmud. In particular, I would like to thank my brother-in-law, Rabbi David Bateman, with whom I have spent countless hours discussing methods and principles of teaching Talmud. Sincere appreciation goes to Rabbi Michael Myers and Charlotte Rosenwald, who reviewed and edited the manuscript and made numerous suggestions that have significantly enhanced the presentation of this work. Finally, I would like to thank my wife, Esther, for her constant help and encouragement.

Originally this small book was written as a study guide or companion resource for the school-age student of Talmud. However, with the passing of time and the explosion of classes and works to help guide the adult beginner-student of Talmud, this work can serve a much broader population. It is my hope that—to whatever measure—this book will assist individuals in their desire to better comprehend the words and ideas of our blessed sages.

I commend Jason Aronson Publishers and its editorial department for its professionalism in making this work worthy of publication.

Heshvan, 5757
S. A. Berman
West Orange, NJ

INTRODUCTION

The Talmud is a tightly woven piece of literature with a unique format and style. It may even be compared to a secret code requiring careful deciphering to unlock its secrets. Once the code is broken, however, its contents become accessible and its treasures are there for the taking. What is the code? How does one break it? This Glossary is designed to help answer those questions while aiding students to, ultimately, learn Talmud independently.

A most fascinating feature of the Talmud's literary style is the unique manner of using Aramaic, the language of the Talmud. Often words or groups of words go beyond their literal meaning and connote a precise function as well. The word תְּנַן, for example, literally means "we learned." However, its full meaning is "we learned in a mishna." The function here is to introduce a mishna into the ongoing disj17cussion. Students previously exposed to Talmud may recognize this term. What many students fail to recognize is that numerous terms like תְּנַן appear throughout the Talmud. These terms are used frequently and repeatedly. A student's ability to learn the Talmud is greatly facilitated by the recognition of these key terms.

The שַׁקְלָא וְטַרְיָא—"give and take"—is another important literary feature of the Talmud. Each section of Talmud may be broken down into the individual statements of the sages as they discuss and argue the issues before them. Each of these statements has a specific function: One may be to ask a question, the next to answer the question, another to disprove the answer with a Torah source, while yet another may come to reject that source, and so on. Because each individual term carries with it a specific function as well, recognition of these terms is often the key to understanding the individual statements.

Let the following section of Talmud from the beginning of Tractate Ta'anit suffice to illustrate the point.

התיבה ביו"ט האחרון של חג האחרון מזכיר
הראשון אינו מזכיר יביו"ט הראשון של פסח
הראשון מזכיר האחרון אינו מזכיר : גמ'
*תנא |היכא קאי דקתני מאימתי |תנא |התם
קאי דקתני *מזכירין גבורות גשמים בתחיית
המתים ישואלין בברכת השנים יוהבדלה
בחונן הדעת וקתני מאימתי מזכירין גבורות
גשמים |וליתני |התם מ"ש דשבקיה עד |הכא|
|אלא |תנא| מראש השנה סליק |דתנן |*ובחג
נידונין על המים |ואיידי דתנא ובחג נידונין
על המים |תנא| מאימתי מזכירין גבורות
גשמים |וליתני מאימתי מזכידין על הגשמים
מאי גבורות גשמים א"ר יוחנן מפני שיורדין

Note the straight lines inserted within the body of the text. The lines serve to separate the individual statements within the dialogue. The boxed words are terms. Notice that every statement has in it at least one term. Remember, too, that each statement performs a function in the Talmud. It now becomes clear that the terms often uncover what those functions are. Now that the student has determined what the Talmud "wants to do," that is, the function, it becomes a much simpler task to understand what the Talmud is "trying to say," that is, the context.

There have been numerous books written as introductions to the Talmud, both classical and contemporary, in Hebrew and in English, as well as in other languages. They may cover subjects such as historical background, chronologies, talmudic and halachic principles, forms of analysis, weights and measurement, common vocabulary, and Aramaic grammar. Some have been written for the advanced student, while others have been written for the beginner. I do not wish to duplicate the work of others. Therefore, I encourage beginning students to refer to *The Gateway to Learning* by Eliyahu Krupnick and *Aiding Talmud Study* by Aryeh Carmell for the above-mentioned areas. Also, the ספר מילים Dictionary, compiled by Marcus Jastrow, is the most comprehensive Aramaic-English dictionary available for Talmud study. A relatively new dictionary, *The Practical Talmud Dictionary* by Yaakov Frank, is an important contribution for the student of Talmud.

This glossary is written with the English-speaking student in mind and as a reference for the teacher. It is a complete glossary of Talmud "terms" in English. The Talmud student should find much guidance in his or her studies by properly utilizing the Glossary. The importance of reading the sections "Using the Glossary," "To the Student," and "To the Teacher" (for teachers) cannot be overemphasized.

PART I
TALMUD TERMS

USING THE GLOSSARY

Things to know:

1 Terms are listed according to אָלֶף בֵּית.
2 Each term is placed along the right margin in boldface.
3 Directly across from each term is its literal translation in quotation marks along the left margin.
4 A = application.
  The application is the term's function as employed in the Talmud. The application generally goes beyond the simple literal translation.
5 L = Literary structure.
  A literary structure represents a broader use of a term. Terms may be found in particular syntactical patterns or in specific combinations with other terms and words. Terms are fixed. That is to say, terms are used according to their applications. (Exceptions do exist. Rashi generally points them out.) Literary structures are not fixed. Thus, a term may be utilized on one occasion in a specific literary structure, but not utilized in another. Therefore, only a few examples of literary structures have been included as illustrations of terms in their broader usage.

6   "Same," "similar," and "related" are employed with refer-
     ence to other terms as they relate to the term under
     discussion. "Same" means that the applications are
     identical or nearly identical. "Similar" means closely
     connected in application, but important, sometimes
     subtle, differences exist. "Related" means that the
     terms are usually related linguistically but retain sepa-
     rate applications, which may be, at times, close in
     meaning.

7   A Tana is a sage who lived during the period of the
     Mishna, approximately 100 B.C.E. to 200 C.E. A tanaitic
     source refers to Mishna, Braita, or Tosefta.

8   An Amora is a sage who lived during the period of the
     Talmud, approximately 200 C.E. to 500 C.E. An amoraic
     statement is a quote from a sage during the period of
     the Talmud.

9   "Halacha" refers to Jewish law. "A halacha" refers to a
     specific Jewish law.

To the Student

This Glossary is meant as an aid in learning Talmud. For any aid to be helpful, one must know its correct use. The following few steps will help you in using the Glossary to your best advantage:

1 Read the Introduction.
2 Read the section entitled "Things to Know."
3 When learning a section of Talmud and confronting a word or phrase you think may be a term, take the chance—look it up.
4 Read the term carefully. Say it out loud. Ask yourself if the definition makes sense. If it does not, ask your teacher to clarify the meaning.
5 Make a little mark with your pen, to the right of the term, after looking it up for the first time. This may help you to remember when looking it up on later occasions.
6 Try committing these terms to memory. You should be able to recognize them as they appear in the Talmud.
7 Memorize the terms as you see them used in the Talmud. To learn the terms in isolation from talmudic context may be a futile waste of your precious time.

To the Teacher

The following steps should direct you in using this Glossary with your students to the fullest advantage:

1 Read the Introduction.
2 Read the section entitled "Things to Know."
3 Read the section entitled "To the Student."
4 Make sure you have your students read the Introduction and the sections entitled "Things to Know" and "To the Student."
5 Before teaching any new section of Talmud, introduce the terms that appear for the first time.
6 Read the definition out loud. Make sure your students comprehend the meaning of each term. Sometimes the definitions will appear too technical for them. Be sure to illustrate the definitions with concrete examples.
7 Have the students make a mark, with their pens, to the right side of every new term they learn. This will indicate to them the terms they will be responsible for knowing.
8 Have students keep their own glossary of terms. Let them add to it as they learn new terms. By having them write out the definitions in their own words,

you better the chance that they truly comprehend the meaning of the definitions.

9   Teach the terms as they appear in the context of the Talmud that you are learning in class. To teach them lists of terms unrelated to anything they are learning will almost certainly lead to poor retention and could create negative feelings toward the Glossary.

10   Note that the definitions are based on many sources, both classical and modern. There are often disagreements as to the precise meaning of a given term. Exceptions also arise. At times you may find a term defined too narrowly; other times, too generally. The approach taken here is to help the English-speaking student as much as possible. Concern about how often a term is used in a specific way, while not over-burdening a student with too narrow a definition, were considered in assigning definitions. If you take issue with a particular definition, do not hesitate to provide your own.

11   Drill the terms in the beginning minutes of every class (while taking attendance or handing back papers). This quick review is a good way to ensure the retention of the terms your students have already learned.

GLOSSARY OF TERMS

"Greater than this"
אַדְרַבָּא

A. Introducing a reason why the contrary is true.
Related: אֵיפּוּךְ

"On which"
אַהֵיָיא

A. Questioning to what case or circumstances
the statement refers.

"Establishing" (particular application)
אוֹקִימְתָּא

A. Determination of special circumstances or
conditions under which a statement in a tanaitic
source holds true.

"He learns the way of the matter"
אוֹרְחָא דְמִלְתָא קָתָנֵי

A. Indicating that nothing more than face
value should be derived from the tanaitic

9

source. The example merely reflects a
common application of the law.

"Sage X goes according   (וְ) אָזְדָא Sage X לְטַעְמֵיה
to his reasoning"

A.   Opening to a related statement said
elsewhere by the same sage. This statement
is consistent with the statement he already
said in this discussion.

"It was asked to them" (the sages)   אִיבָּעְיָא לְהוּ
("It was asked to him")   (אִיבָּעְיָא לֵיה)

A.   Introducing a question of information
in anticipation of an answer.

"If you want, I can say"   אִי בָּעֵית אֵימָא

A.   Offering an alternative explanation,
clarification, or version.

L.   אִי בָּעֵית אֵימָא . . . אִי בָּעֵית אֵימָא

"If you want, I can say (quote) . . . אִי בָּעֵית אֵימָא קְרָא
a biblical verse . . .

If you want, I can say a
logical inference . . . . "   . . . וְאִי בָּעֵית אֵימָא סְבָרָא

A.   Opening of two proofs or explanations
of the same matter. One proof is based on a
biblical verse, the other on logic.

"(And) the other" (וְ)אִידָךְ

A.   When not used in its literal sense, this
term asks how a sage will be able to reconcile
the proof just raised in support of the opposing
sage's view.

"If (this is) so" אִי הָכִי

A.   Opening to a question on the previously
stated explanation or answer, as in the following
formula: אִי הָכִי, If (this is) so that ... then ...?

"Since that . . . . " אַיְידֵי דְ . . .

A.   Opening to an explanation for the need
of an apparent superfluous or irrelevant case
within a tanaitic source.

L.   אַיְידֵי דְבָעֵי לְמִיתְנָא סֵיפָא . . . תְּנָא נַמִי רֵישָׁא
Related: צְרִיכוּתָא, צְרִיכָא, לָא צְרִיכָא לֵיה

"There is (this difference) between them" אִיכָּא בֵּינַיְיהוּ

A.   Introducing a clarification of a practical
halachic distinction between two opinions.

L.   מַאי בֵּינַיְיהוּ ... אִיכָּא בֵּינַיְיהוּ

"There were those that say . . . " אִיכָּא דְאָמְרֵי . . .

A.   Opening to an alternative version.
Same: אִיכָּא דִמְפָרְשֵׁי הָכִי
Similar: דָּבָר אַחֵד, אָמְרֵי לַהּ, אִי תֵימָא, אִי נֵימָא

"There are those that explain it like this."

אִיכָּא דִּמְפָרְשֵׁי הָכִי

A.   Opening to an alternative version.

Same: אִיכָּא דְּאָמְרֵי

Similar: דָּבָר אַחֵר, אָמְרִי לַהּ, אִי חֵימָא, אִי נֵימָא

"There is to say"

אִיכָּא לְמֵימַר

A.   See: מַאי אִיכָּא לְמֵימַר

"If we will say"

אִילֵּימָא

A.   Raises a supposition that is later rejected.

Same: לֵימָא, וְכִי חֵימָא, הֲוָה אֲמִינָא, אִי נַמֵּי, אִם תִּמְצֵי לוֹמַר

קָא סָלְקָא דַעְתָּךְ, סָבְרוּהָ, נֵימָא, מַהוּ דְּתֵימָא

Related: סָבוּר מִינָהּ, אֵימָא

"Say . . . "

אֵימָא . . .

A.   (1) Opening to a question or emendation
of a previous explanation by raising an
alternative understanding immediately rejected.
The Gemara then generally proves why the
original explanation is necessarily correct.

A.   (2) In the common literary phrase of
אֵימָא רֵישָׁא, one needs to explain as follows: Read
the first part of the tanaitic source in order to
see how your explanation of the latter part
is incorrect.

L.   . . . אֵימָא סֵיפָא . . . לָא חֵימָא . . . אֶלָּא אֵימָא

Similar: תְּנִי

"I would say" (I would admit)   אֵימוּר

A.   Questioning the previous statement by demonstrating its restricted use.

"Yes, this is also so (true)"   אִין, הָכִי נַמֵי

A.   This term indicates that a sage agrees with the point made by the question. However, the sage retains his original viewpoint in favor of the question by either (1) interpreting the circumstances of the case in such a way that the question does not apply or (2) introducing an alternative source that contradicts the conclusions drawn from the first one.

"Is it not so that . . . . !?!"   אֵינוֹ דִין שֶׁ . . . ! ? !

A.   Conclusion to a קַל וָחוֹמֶר *Kal veChomer.* The logic of a קַל וָחוֹמֶר is as follows: If this is true by the less obvious case, is it not so that in the more obvious case it must certainly be true?

Similar: . . . עַל אַחַת כַּמָה וְכַמָה, כָּל שֶׁכֵּן שֶׁ

Related: דִין

"Is it so!?!"   אִינִי ! ? !

A.   Opening to a proof showing that the previous statement is incorrect. The term is read rhetorically.

"If (you want), we can say . . . "   . . . אִי נֵימָא

A.   An opening to an alternative explanation.

Similar: אִיכָּא דְאָמְרִי, אִיכָּא דִמְפָרְשֵׁי הָכִי, אִי חֵימָא
דָּבָר אַחֵר, אָמְרִי לָהּ

"Switch it around"   אֵיפּוֹךְ

A.   (1) Introduces a resolution to a
contradiction within an argument by
switching around the names of the sages
with the views they state. As in the formula:
"Sage X says . . . (A) and Sage Y says . . . (B)."
Switch it around to say: "Sage Y says . . . (A)
and Sage X says . . . (B)."

Same: מוּחְלֶפֶת הַשִּׁיטָה

A.   (2) Suggests that the opposite of the
previous interpretation be made.

L.   אֵיפּוֹךְ אֲנָא, מִסְתַּבְּרָא

Related: אַדְרַבָּא

"It is needed for it"   אִיצְטְרִיכָא לֵיהּ

A.   Opening to an explanation for the
need of an apparent superfluous or irrelevant
case.

Similar: צְרִיכָתָא, צְרִיכָא, לָא צְרִיכָא

Related: . . . אַיְּדֵי דְ

"He has" (accepts)   אִית לֵיהּ

A.   Indicating that a given sage accepts
the view of another sage.

"He asked against him"   אִיתִיבֵיה
A.   One Amora raises questions against
another, usually from a tanaitic source
while occasionally from a biblical verse.
Similar: מֵיתִיבִי
Related: תְּיוּבְתָּא

"If you want to say . . . "   . . . אִיתֵימָא
A.   Introducing an alternative version as to
who authored the statement.
Similar: אִיכָּא דִמְפָרְשִׁי הָכִי, אִיכָּא דְאָמְרֵי, אִי נֵימָא
דָבָר אַחֵר, אָמְרִי לַהּ

"It was said"   אִיתְּמַר
A.   Indicating a statement from the Amoraim,
usually of a dispute.
L.   אִיתְּמַר נַמֵי הָכִי
אִיתְּמַר עֲלָהּ

"But . . . "   . . . אֶלָּא
A.   This term acts as a transition between the
rejection of a previous interpretation and the
introduction of a new one. This is only so when
אֶלָּא stands by itself and not when it is part of a
compound phrase such as אֶלָּא מַאי or אֶלָּא אִם כֵּן

"But is it not . . . !?!"   אֶלָּא לָאו . . . !?!
A.   This term is rhetorical, implying: "This
is definitely so."

"But [from] now" (But according to this)   אֶלָּא מֵעַתָּה

A.   This term begins to indicate that based
on what was just previously said, the following
inference must be concluded. This inference,
however, would prove to be impossible or
ridiculous. Therefore, the previous interpretation
must be rejected.

Related: אִם אִיתָא

"If there is"   אִם אִיתָא

A.   A statement of inference. According to
the preceding statement the following
inference should be made.

Related: אֶלָּא מֵעַתָּה

"Translator"   אָמוֹרָא

A.   Reference to an amoraic sage.

"Some say it"   אָמְרֵי לַהּ

A.   Introducing an alternative version or
author of a statement.

Similar: אִי נֵימָא, אִיכָּא דִמְפָרְשֵׁי הָכִי, אִיכָּא דְאָמְרֵי
דָבָר אַחֵר, אֵיתֵימָא

"Master said"   אָמַר מָר

A.   Indicating a quote from a previous
section of Talmud. The Talmud now deals
with an aspect of the previous discussion
that, when originally raised, would have

been off the subject.
Same: גוּפָא

"If you can (are able to)   אִם תִּמְצֵי לוֹמַר . . .
find, say . . . "
A.   (1) Rejection of a possible explanation
by first raising it as a possibility, then
showing how it is incorrect or unacceptable.
Similar: לֵימָא, וְכִי תֵימָא, הֲוָה אֲמִינָא, אִילֵימָא
קָא סָלְקָא דַעְתָּךְ, סְבַרוּהָ, מַהוּ דְתֵימָא, נֵימָא
Related: סָבוּר מִינָהּ, אֵימָא
A.   (2) When the Talmud considers one of
two previous possibilities to a problem, the
following question may be raised, as in the
following formula:
"Question, Answer 1, Answer 2. אִם תִּמְצֵי לוֹמַר
Answer 1 (If you say Answer 1) then ask this
question . . . . ?"

<u>אוֹת ב</u>

"Question"   בָּעְיָא
A.   See אִיבַּעְיָא לְהוּ

"It is good"   בִּשְׁלָמָא
A.   (1) Questioning an Amora by
demonstrating that a halacha is in conflict
with his view, while the same halacha is
perfectly in line with the opposing Amora's
view. The term first introduces the Amora
consistent with the halacha.
L.   אֶלָּא לְ Sage Y . . מַאי אִיכָּא לְמֵימַר

בִּשְׁלָמָא לְ Sage X . . .
Similar: תִּינַח, תָּנִיחָא

A.   (2) Questioning an explanation by
demonstrating that, although one aspect
is in keeping with a halacha or logic,
another is not.

L.   ? . . . אִי אָמְרַתְּ בִּשְׁלָמָא . . . אֶלָּא אִי אָמְרַתְּ

אוֹת ג

"Itself"   גּוּפָא

A.   Indicating a quote from a previous
section of Talmud. The Talmud now deals
with an issue of the previous discussion
that, when originally raised, would have
been off the subject.

Same: אֲמַר מָר

אוֹת ד

"Another matter"   דָּבָר אַחֵר

A.   (1) Introduces another answer or explanation.

Similar: אִיכָּא דְּמְפָרְשֵׁי הָכִי, אִיכָּא דְּאַמְרֵי
אָמְרֵי לַהּ, אִיתֵּימָא, אִי נֵימָא

A.   (2) Euphemism for (a) pig, (b) sexual
relations, (c) Tzarat (biblical skin disease),
(d) money.

"Law"   דִּין

A.   When not implying its literal meaning,
this term indicates that logical reasoning
should be employed.

L.   הֲלֹא דִין הוּא

Related: ... שֶׁ אֵינוֹ דִין

אוֹת ה

"But" or "This" or "That"   הָא

"But he said"   הָא אָמַר (הָאָמַר)

"But it was learned"   הָא תַּנְיָא (הָתַנְיָא)

"But we learned"   הָא תְּנַן (הָתְנַן)

A. The word הָא or prefix הָ indicates that
a question will be raised from the following
source. In the case of הָא תְּנַן it is a question
from the mishna. In the case of הָא תַּנְיָא it is a
question from a braita or tosefta. In הָא אָמַר
it is a question from a sage's statement,
usually that of an Amora. When not
mentioned in one of these three ways,
it should be translated as "this" or
"that," referring simply to an object
or subject.

"This, what is it?"   הַאי מַאי

A. Questioning how two things just
mentioned can be compared.

Similar: כְּמַאי

"It (the mishna) is (speaking) in . . . "   הַהִיא בְּ . . .

A. Answering a question against a mishna
by explaining its application in more restricted
circumstances.

"I would have said"   הֲוָה אֲמִינָא

A.   Raises a supposition that is later rejected.

L.   הֲוָה אֲמִינָא . . . קָא מַשְׁמַע לָן

Similar: לֵימָא, וְכִי תֵּימָא, אִם תִּמְצֵי לוֹמַר, אִילֵימָא

קָא סָלְקָא דַעְתָּךְ, סְבָרוּהָ, נֵימָא, מַהוּ דְתֵימָא

Related: סְבוּר מִינָה, אֵימָא

(1) "So it is the law . . . "   . . . הוּא הַדִּין

A.   Pointing out that the previously
established halacha is equally valid in
the following case.

(2) "This is . . . . " (identical with . . .)   . . . הוּא הַדִּין

A.   Questions the necessity of a statement
whose main idea seems either (1) contained
within another statement or (2) stated explicitly
elsewhere.

Similar: מַאי לְמֵימְרָא . . . לָמָה לִי, הַיְינוּ . . .

מִיבַּעְיָא, מַאי קָמַשְׁמַע לָן

Related: מַאי רְבוּתָא, הַיְינוּ הָךְ

"That is . . . !"   הַיְינוּ . . . !

A.   Read in astonishment, this term objects
to a case or statement that appears identical
with a previously stated case or statement.

Similar: מַאי לְמֵימְרָא . . . לָמָה לִי, הוּא הַדִּין

מִיבַּעְיָא, מַאי קָמַשְׁמַע לָן

Related: מַאי רְבוּתָא, הַיְינוּ הָךְ

L.   הַיְינוּ _____ הַיְינוּ _____

"This is (identical with) that"
A. Questions the need for stating two laws when they both appear identical in principle.

Related: ‏מַאי לְמֵימְרָא ... לָמָה לִי, הַיְינוּ ...‏
‏מִיבַּעְיָא, מַאי רְבוּתָא, מַאי קָמַשְׁמַע לָן‏

‏הַיְינוּ הָךְ‏

"Where does it stand?" (come from)
A. Asking what basis there is for the halacha stated in the tanaitic source.

‏הֵיכָא קָאֵי?‏

"How is it similar?"
(How is it to be understood?)
A. Asking for clarification of the case, or circumstances of some issue.

‏הֵיכִי דָמֵי?‏

"How do you find it?"
A. Questioning if there is any practical application of a halacha.

Related: ‏מִי מַשְׁכַּחַתְּ לֵיהּ‏

‏הֵיכִי מַשְׁכַּחַתְּ לֵיהּ?‏

"How does he say?"
(What does he mean?)
A. Asking under what circumstances or case a sage's statement applies.

‏הֵיכִי קָאָמַר?‏

"Here"/"There"
A. "Here" refers to the main tanaitic source

‏הָכָא\הָתָם‏

under discussion. "There" refers to an outside
tanaitic source brought in to elucidate
further the present discussion. Sometimes
the respective terms are used to
differentiate one thing from another.

"Here, with what are we dealing?" הָכָא בְּמַאי עָסְקִינַן
A.   A rhetorical question that limits the
application of a tanaitic source. Usually
this is in response to a previous question
raised upon the source.

"How is this so?" הָכִי הַשְׁתָּא?
A.   Questions the Talmud's logic in
comparing two things and shows how
they are dissimilar.
L.   הָכִי הַשְׁתָּא? . . . הָתָם . . . הָכָא . . . ?
Same: מִי דָּמֵי
Related: הַאי מַאי

"Like this he/it says" הָכִי קָאָמַר
A.   Introducing a statement that reinterprets
the source under discussion. Usually this is in
response to a question raised upon the
tanaitic source.
Similar: תְּנֵי, הָכִי קָתָנֵי

"(In) this (manner), he learns"
הָכִי קָתָּנֵי

A.   Introducing a restating or rephrasing of
the tanaitic source. Usually this is in response
to a question raised upon the source.

L.   חַסּוֹרֵי מְחַסְּרָא, וְהָכִי קָתָּנֵי

Similar: תָּנֵי, הָכִי קָאָמַר

"It is good . . . "
הָנִיחָא . . .

A.   Questioning an Amora by demonstrating
that a tanaitic source is in conflict with his
view, while the same source is perfectly in line
with the opposing Amora's view. The term first
introduces the Amora consistent with the
tanaitic source.

L.   הָנִיחָא לְ Sage X . . . אֶלָּא לְ Sage Y . . . מַאי אִיכָּא לְמֵימַר?

Same: בִּשְׁלָמָא

Similar: תִּינַח

"These words"
תָּנֵי מִילֵי (ה״מ, הנ״מ)

A.   Introducing a statement that limits
the application of a case, statement, or
halacha.

"Now that you have come to this . . . "
הַשְׁתָּא דַּאֲתֵית לְהָכִי . . .

A.   With this conclusion or solution,
other questions can be resolved

without the need to rely on alternative
answers.

הָתָם   See הָכָא\הָתָם

<u>אות ו</u>

וְאֵידְךְ   See אֵידְךְ

וְאָזְדָא Sage X לְטַעֲמֵיה   See אָזְדָא Sage X לְטַעֲמֵיה

וְהָא תַּנְיָא   See הָא

"And if you were to say . . . "   . . . וְכִי תֵּימָא

A. Raises a supposition that is later rejected.

L. . . . וְכִי תֵּימָא . . . קָא מַשְׁמַע לַן

Similar: הֲוָה אֲמִינָא, אִם תִּמְצֵי לוֹמַר, אִילֵימָא

סְבָרוּהָ, נֵימָא, מַהוּ דְּתֵימָא, לֵימָא

קָא סָלְקָא דַּעְתָּךְ

Related: סָבוּר מִינָהּ, אֵימָא

"(And) it is not it" (It is not so)   וְלֹא הִיא

A. Introduces a rejection to the previous
statement.

וְלִיטַעְמָךְ   See לִיטַעְמָךְ ! ? !

וּרְמִינְהוּ   See רָמִינְהוּ

"(Not only) this (case), even that (case) is learned"

זוֹ אַף זוֹ קָתָנֵי

A.   The seemingly redundant case in the Mishna can be attributed to style. The Mishna begins with the more obvious case and moves to the less obvious one.

Related: זוֹ וְאֵין צָרִיךְ לוֹמַר זוֹ קָתָנֵי

"This (case is needed), and that (case) is not necessary to be learned."

זוֹ וְאֵין צָרִיךְ לוֹמַר זוֹ קָתָנֵי

A.   The seemingly redundant case in the Mishna can be attributed to style. The Mishna begins with the less obvious case and moves to the more obvious one.

Related: זוֹ אַף זוֹ קָתָנֵי

"It (the tanaitic source) is deficient . . . "

. . . חַסּוֹרֵי מְחַסְּרָא

A.   See הָכִי קָתָנֵי

"You could say . . . "
(Short for אַתָּה יָכוֹל לוֹמַר)

. . . יָכוֹל

A.   Raises a false conclusion a person might make if it were not for an inference to be derived from a biblical verse.

L.   . . . יָכוֹל . . . תַּלְמוּד לוֹמַר

<u>אוֹת כ</u>

"As it was learned . . . "   . . . כִּדְתַנְיָא
A.   A braita or tosefta is introduced as a
support to a certain opinion.

"The entire world" (agrees)   כּוּלֵי עָלְמָא
A.   All sages of this talmudic passage
agree on a given point.

L.   כּוּלֵי עָלְמָא לָא פְּלִיגֵי

. . . בְּ מַחְלוֹקֶת (case A) אֲבָל בּ (case B) . . . דְ מוֹדֵי עָלְמָא כּוּלֵי

See וְכִי תֵּימָא   כִּי תֵּימָא

"Certainly then . . . "   . . . כָּל שֶׁכֵּן שֶׁ
A.   Conclusion to a קַל וָחוֹמֶר *Kal veChomer.*
The logic of a קַל וָחוֹמֶר is as follows: If the
ruling is such in case A, "certainly then" in
case B the ruling must be so!

Similar: . . . שֶׁ דִין אֵינוֹ וְכַמָּה, כַּמָּה אַחַת עַל

"Toward where?" (are you turning)   כְּלַפֵּי לָיָּא
A.   An exclamatory remark on an
explanation that appears to be contrary
to logic.

See קְרִי   כְּתִיב

"Like the tanaitic sages"
כְּתַנָּאֵי

A.   The Talmud indicates that the present Amoraic disagreement is based on an earlier tanaitic disagreement.

Same: תַּנָּאֵי הִיא, לֵימָא כְּתַנָּאֵי

<u>אוֹת ל</u>

See וְלָא הִיא
לָא הִיא

"Not (only) this (case) even that (case) is learned"
לָא זוֹ אַף זוֹ קָתָנֵי

A.   See זוֹ אַף זוֹ קָתָנֵי

See . . . כָּל שֶׁכֵּן שֶׁ
לָא כָּל שֶׁכֵּן

"It is not needed, he has said!"
לָא מִיבַּעְיָא קָאָמַר!

A.   This term indicates that a tana seems redundant. The tana begins with a less obvious case and moves to a more obvious one.

Related: מִיבַּעְיָא

"No, it is needed"
לָא, צְרִיכָא

A.   The Talmud explains the necessity for a statement despite its apparent redundancy.

L.   פְּשִׁיטָא! לָא צְרִיכָא

Similar: . . . צְרִיכוּתָא, צְרִיכָא, אִי צְרִיכָא לֵיהּ, אַיְידֵי דְ

Related: . . . לָא צְרִיכָא אֶלָּא

"It is only needed . . . "   ... לָא צְרִיכָא אֶלָּא

A.   Explaining a tanaitic source or halacha in specific circumstances. Usually in response to a question raised upon the source of a halacha.

Related: צְרִיכָא, לָא צְרִיכָא, אִיצְרִיכָא לֵיה, אַיְּדֵי דְ . . . צְרִיכוּתָא

"Sage X did not hear it"   לָא שְׁמִיעַ לֵ Sage X

A.   The sage does not accept a certain opinion. Sometimes it is to be taken literally, in the sense that a sage is not aware of a halacha.

"This is nothing"   לָאו מִילְתָא הִיא

A.   Introducing a rejection of the previously stated opinion.

"According to your reasoning!?!"   (וּ)לִטְעָמֵיךְ! ? ?!

A.   The Talmud shows how the question just raised can be turned around and asked against the same sage who asked the question.

"Let him say" (If he were to say)   לֵימָא

A.   Raises a supposition that is later rejected.

L.   לֵימָא . . . קָא מַשְׁמַע לָן . . .

Similar: וְכִי תֵּימָא, הֲוָה אֲמִינָא, אִם תִּמְצֵי לוֹמַר, אִילֵּימָא

קָא סָלְקָא דַּעְתָּךְ, סָבְרוּהָ, נֵימָא, מַהוּ דְּתֵימָא, לֵימָא

Related: סָבוּר מִינָה, אֵימָא

"Let him say (that it is) like the tanaitic sages"
לֵימָא (נֵימָא) כְּתַנָּאֵי

A. The Talmud shows that this amoraic dispute is based on an earlier tanaitic dispute. Same: תַּנָּאֵי, כְּתַנָּאֵי הִיא

"Let him say that this (source) supports him"
לֵימָא מְסַיֵּיע לֵיה

A. Suggesting a tanaitic source as a support to an Amora's opinion, which is immediately rejected.

"Another version"
לִישָׁנָא אַחֲרִינָא

A. An alternative version, which usually bears some significant difference.

"He should answer"
לִישַׁנֵּי

A. Opening to an answer suggested by the Talmud on behalf of the sage to whom a question was just asked.

"We do not have it"
לֵית לָן בָּה

A. This term shows an instance that a law, taken as a given rule, does not apply.

"Let him teach"
לִיתְנֵי

A. In questioning the version of the tanaitic source, this term suggests an alternative version that is clearer.

See מַאי נָפְקָא מִינָה   לְמַאי נָפְקָא מִינָה

" . . . what (meaning is in this)   ? . . . לָמָה לִי
for me?"
A.   Questioning the need for a case or law
that appears redundant.
Similar: מַאי לְמֵימְרָא, הַיְינוּ . . . הוּא הַדִּין . . .
מִיבָּעְיָא, מַאי קָמַשְׁמַע לָן
Related: מַאי רְבוּתָא, הַיְינוּ הַך

"To cast" (a contradiction)   לְמִירְמָא
A.   Introducing one source to contradict
another source of equal status (i.e., mishna
against mishna, biblical verse against biblical
verse, etc.). Sometimes the contradiction
arises from two opposing statements of the
same sage.
Same: רָמֵי, רוּמְיָא or רְמִינְהוּ

"Actually"   לְעוֹלָם
A.   Opening to a reassertion of a
previously refuted answer. The Talmud
proceeds to answer the questions
previously raised against it.

<u>אוֹת מ</u>

" . . . what is there to say?"   ? מַאי אִיכָּא לְמֵימַר
A.   This term is applied when only
one of two opinions or laws is clear

and understood. The term ends a
statement, questioning the clarity or
understandability of the second
opinion or law.

"Why does case X appear (here)?" מַאי אִירְיָא?

A.   This term questions the specificity
of a stated case within a tanaitic source
when the ruling actually applies more
gcnerally.

L.   . . . מַאי אִירְיָא . . . צְרִיכָא

"What (difference) is there between them?" מַאי בֵּינַייהוּ?

A.   Questioning the halachic distinction
between two cases, statements, or opinions.

L.   מַאי בֵּינַייהוּ . . . אִיכָּא בֵּינַייהוּ

See מַאי נָפְקָא מִינָה

"What about it?" מַאי הָוֵי עֲלַהּ?

A.   At the end of a discussion, this term
requests a final halachic conclusion on a
disputed point, which, as yet, has not
been decided.

"What did you see?" מַאי חֲזֵית?

A.   This term questions why a sage prefers
one particular view over others.

Same: מָה רָאִיתָ

"What is the reason?"   ?מַאי טַעְמָא

A.   Generally this term asks for the Torah source of the halacha. Occasionally it is asking for the reasoning behind a halacha.

"What is it? Is it not . . . . ?"   ? . . . . מַאי, לָאו

A.   This term raises an alternative way of explaining the matter under discussion. It should be read as follows: What is the explanation of X? Should it not be explained thus. . . . The explanation usually is immediately rejected.

"What to say?"   מַאי לְמֵימְרָא

A.   This term questions the statement of a Tana or Amora when it appears obvious or is stated explicitly elsewhere.

Similar: . . . . לָמָה לִי, הַיְינוּ . . . הוּא הַדִין . . . .
מִיבַּעְיָא, מַאי קָא מַשְׁמַע לָן
Related: מַאי רְבוּתָא, הַיְינוּ הָךְ

"What is the implication?"   ?מַאי מַשְׁמַע

A.   This term asks how the halacha is derived from the biblical source. It is applied when the connection is not initially obvious.

"What comes out of it?"   ?מַאי נָפְקָא מִינָה (ל)

A.   Questioning if there is any

practical halachic distinction
between two cases or statements.
Similar: מַאי בֵּינַיְיהוּ
Related: נָפְקָא מִינָא

"What is he saying?"   מַאי קָאָמַר?
A.   This term is applied in order to
ask for further clarification, when a
tanaitic source is unclear.
L.   מַאי קָאָמַר . . . הָכִי קָאָמַר

"What does he teach us?"   מַאי קָא מַשְׁמַע לָן?
A.   The Talmud asks what new teaching
an Amora has to offer by making a
statement already well known or explicit
in another source. If the statement is made
in another source it is usually quoted by
the Talmud.
Similar: מַאי לְמֵימְרָא . . . לָמָה לִי, הַיְינוּ, הוּא הַדִין מִיבַּעְיָא
Related: מַאי רְבוּתָא, הַיְינוּ הָךְ

"What is (the) great (benefit)?"   מַאי רְבוּתָא?
A.   The Talmud asks what more this
stated case has to convey.
Related: לָמָה לִי, הַיְינוּ הָךְ, הַיְינוּ . . . הוּא הַדִין
מִיבַּעְיָא, מַאי קָמַשְׁמַע לָן, מַאי לְמֵימְרָא

"What is the inference?"   מַאי תַלְמוּדָא?
A.   The Talmud questions how a sage
arrives at a halachic conclusion based
on the biblical source he provided.

"The one who says . . . "   ‏. . . מָאן דְּאָמַר‏
A.   The sage who adopts the view of . . .

"Who remembers his (its) name?"   ‏מָאן דְּכַר שְׁמֵיהּ?‏
A.   The Talmud expresses astonishment
when a detail is mentioned in only one of
two parts of a source. To be consistent,
this detail should have been stated in both
parts of the source.

"Who is the Tana?"   ‏מָאן תַּנָּא‏
A.   Leading question to the identification
of a tanaitic source's authorship.

See ‏מִיבַּעְיָא‏   ‏מִבַּעְיָא‏

"Whatever you want"   ‏מָה נַפְשָׁךְ‏
A.   This term introduces difficulties with
both possibilities raised in the preceding
section of Talmud. The effect is to question
and sometimes reject both possibilities.
Same: ‏מִמָּה נַפְשָׁךְ‏

See ‏מַאי חֲזֵית‏   ‏מָה רָאִיתָ‏

"What is it?"   ‏מַהוּ‏
A.   What is the halacha?

"What might you say?"　מַהוּ דְּתֵימָא

A.　Raises a supposition that is later rejected.

L.　מַהוּ דְּתֵימָא . . . קָא מַשְׁמַע לָן

Similar:　וְכִי תֵימָא, הֲוָה אֲמִינָא, אִם תִּמְצֵי לוֹמַר, אִילֵימָא,
קָא סָלְקָא דַעְתָּךְ, סְבָרוּהָ, נֵימָא, מַהוּ דְּתֵימָא, לֵימָא

Related:　סָבוּר מִינָה, אֵימָא

"From where do you get this?"　מְהֵיכָא תֵיתֵי?

A.　The Talmud has just pointed out that
one may make a mistake if it were not for
a teaching derived from a Torah source.
This term questions the premise that one
would be mistaken if it were not for the
biblical teaching.

"The opinion is reversed"　מוּחְלֶפֶת הַשִּׁיטָה

A.　This term resolves a contradiction
within a dispute between two sages by
reversing the name of each Sage with
the opinion he expresses. Therefore, if
Sage X was previously reported to have
said (A), and Sage Y was reported to have
said (B), say instead that Sage X said (B)
and Sage Y said (A).

Same:　A. (1) אִיפּוּךְ

"Is there anything like this?"　מִי אִיכָּא מִידֵּי?

A.　The practical relevance of the halacha

is brought into question. This term is read
rhetorically.

"Is it similar?"   ?מִי דָמֵי

A.   This term questions the Talmud's logic
in comparing two things and shows how
they are dissimilar. This term is read rhetorically.

L.   . . . וְהָתָם . . . הָכָא ?מִי דָמֵי

Same: הָכִי הַשְׁתָּא

Related: הַאי מַאי

"Who finds it?"   ?מִי מַשְׁכַּחַתְּ לֵיה

A.   Rhetorically, this term questions
the applicability of a case or law stated
in the tanaitic source.

Related: הֵיכִי מַשְׁכַּחַתְּ לֵיה

"It is needed?"   ?מִיבַּעְיָא

A.   This term questions the need for the
former statement, since it seems obvious
or already known through a previous
statement. The term is read rhetorically.

Similar: הַיְינוּ, הוּא הַדִּין

מַאי קָמַשְׁמַע לָן, מַאי לְמֵימְרָא . . . לָמָה לִי

Related: מַאי רְבוּתָא, לָא מִיבַּעְיָא קָאָמַר, הַיְינוּ הַךְ

"Statement"   מֵימְרָא
A.   A statement from an Amora.

See לְמֵירְמָא   מִירְמָא

"They ask"   מֵיתִיבִי
A.   This term introduces a tanaitic source
in objection to an Amora's statement
by anonymous sages of the Talmud.
Similar: אֵיתִיבֵיה
Related: תִּיּוּבְתָּא

"It follows"   מִכְּלָל
A.   A deduction is made based on the
previous statement.

"From what!"   מִמַּאי!
A.   This term questions the basis of a
statement, or how two things are compared.
Similar: הַאי מַאי

See מַה נַפְשָׁךְ   מִמַּה נַפְשָׁךְ

"Where are these   מְנָא הָנֵי מִילֵּי? (מְנָהָנֵי מִילֵּי, מה״מ)
words from?"
A.   The Talmud asks for the Torah source

of the previously stated halacha.

Same: מְנָלָן, מְנַיִין

"From where do we (get this)?"   מְנָא לָן (מְנָלָן, מנ״ל)

A.   See מְנָא הָנֵי מִילֵי?

L.   מְנָא לָן? _____ ל , _____ אַשְׁכְּחַן ל

"Who is it?"   מַנִּי?

A.   This term asks for the author of the
statement under discussion.

"From where?"   מְנַיִין?

A.   See מְנָא הָנֵי מִילֵי

"From where?"   מְנָלָן?

A.   Same as מְנָא הָנֵי מִילֵי

L.   מְנָלָן? (case B) ... (case A) אַשְׁכְּחַן

מְסַיֵּיע לֵיהּ   See לֵימָא מְסַיֵּיע לֵיהּ

"It makes sense"   מִסְתַּבְּרָא

A.   It follows logically that ...

"The west"   מַעֲרְבָא

A.   This term refers to the land of Israel.
Israel is located west of Babylonia. Since
the Talmud was written in Babylonia, Israel
is referred to simply as "the west."

"From now"

מֵעַתָּה

A.   This term questions the previous
statement. The Talmud establishes that,
based upon what was previously said,
the following logical conclusion should
be drawn. This conclusion, however, is
unacceptable.

"It (the source) is distorted"

מְשַׁבְּשְׁתָּא הִיא

A.   This term concludes, in response to
difficulties raised against a braita, that
the braita is, in fact, distorted and
unreliable.

"Teaches"

מַתְנֵי

A.   Introducing a teaching from a tanaitic source.

"Teaching"

מַתְנִיתָא

A.   Reference to a braita as opposed to
מַתְנִיתִין, which refers to a mishna.

"Our teaching"

מַתְנִיתִין

A.   Reference to a mishna as opposed to
מַתְנִיתָא, which refers to a braita. Occasionally
מַתְנִיתִין refers to the mishna upon which this
very section of Talmud is based.

"He asks on it"

מַתְקִיף לַהּ

A.   A sage asks a question based purely on logic.

אוֹת נ

"Let it be" (assume that)   נְהִי
A.   This term introduces an assumption upon
which the following discussion will rest.

See הָנִיחָא   נִיחָא

"Let us say"   נֵימָא
A.   Raises a supposition that is later rejected.
L.   נֵימָא . . . קָא מַשְׁמַע לָן . . .
Similar: וְכִי תֵּימָא, הֲוָה אֲמִינָא, אִם תִּמְצֵי לוֹמַר, אִילֵימָא
קָא סָלְקָא דַעְתָּךְ, סְברוּהַ, מַהוּ דְתֵימָא,
לֵימָא
Related: סָבוּר מִינָהּ, אֵימָא

"It comes out for him" (he derives)   נָפְקָא לֵיה
A.   Introduces a biblical verse upon which
a sage derives the halacha under discussion.

"That which comes out of it"   נָפְקָא מִינָה
A.   A practical halachic distinction is made
between two cases or statements.
Related: מַאי נָפְקָא מִינָה
Similar: אִיכָּא בֵּינַיְיהוּ

"Grasp" (adopt) [We adopt]   נָקֵט [נָקְטִינַן]
A.   Introduces an accepted tradition.

"It is understood from this"   סָבוּר מִינָה

A.   An incorrect conclusion is drawn
from a source that will later be disproven.
Related: הֲוָה אֲמִינָא, אִם תִּמְצֵי לוֹמַר
נֵימָא, מַהוּ דְתֵימָא, לֵימָא, וְכִי תֵימָא
קָא סָלְקָא דַעְתָּךְ, סְבַרוּהָ

"Thought"   סְבָרָא

A.   An idea arrived at by logical reasoning.

"They understood it"   סְבַרוּהָ

A.   Raises a supposition held by anonymous
sages that is later rejected.
Similar: וְכִי תֵימָא, הֲוָה אֲמִינָא, אִם תִּמְצֵי לוֹמַר, אִילֵימָא
קָא סָלְקָא דַעְתָּךְ, נֵימָא, מַהוּ דְתֵימָא, לֵימָא
Related: סָבוּר מִינָה, אֵימָא

"Support"   סִיַּעְתָּא

A.   Usually this term introduces a tanaitic
source as a support to an Amora's opinion.
Occasionally it introduces a purely logical
argument as the support.

"The end" (part)   סֵיפָא

A.   Reference to a latter part of a tanaitic

source or biblical verse as opposed to רֵישָׁא,
which refers to the first part.

סָלְקָא דַעְתָּךְ   See קָא סָלְקָא דַעְתָּךְ

<u>אוֹת ע</u>

"Until here (this point),   עַד כָּאן לָא . . .
no (it is not) . . . "
A.   This term introduces a qualification of
the halacha or dispute under discussion.
L.   . . . אֲבָל הָכָא . . . . עַד כָּאן לָא קָאָמַר פְּלוֹנִי הָתָם אֶלָּא

"How much more so?"   עַל אַחַת כַּמָּה וְכַמָּה
A.   Conclusion to a קַל וָחוֹמֶר *Kal*
veChomer. The logic of קַל וָחוֹמֶר is as
follows: If this is true by the less
obvious case, how much more so
must it be true in a more obvious case?
Similar: אֵינוֹ דִין שׁ . . . ! ? !

<u>אוֹת פ</u>

"Refutation"   פִּירְכָא
A.   Introduction to a refutation, usually
of a קַל וָחוֹמֶר *Kal veChomer.* (For the logic
of עַל אַחַת כַּמָּה וְכַמָּה see קַל וָחוֹמֶר)

"Obvious!"   פְּשִׁיטָא!
A.   (1) Expresses astonishment as to
why the Tana or Amora bothered to state
what is so obvious.

L.   ... **פְּשִׁיטָא! לָא, צְרִיכָא**

A.   (2) Introduces a case (or cases) about
which there is no question. What follows is
a similar case (or cases) about which questions
may be raised.

Similar: **בִּשְׁלָמָא**

אוֹת צ

"It is necessary"   **צְרִיכָא**

A.   The Talmud introduces the reasoning
as to the necessity for the statement or case
in question, despite its apparent redundancy
or obvious nature.

Similar: **צְרִיכוּתָא, לָא צְרִיכָא, אִצְטְרִכָא לֵיהּ**

Related: ... ד **אַיְידֵי**

אוֹת ק

"He/it lets us hear" (teaches us)   **קָא מַשְׁמַע לָן**
                                   [קָמַשְׁמַע לָן, קמ״ל]

A.   This term draws upon the tanaitic
source under discussion in order to reject
an erroneous supposition, as in the formula:
Let us say supposition X, **קָא מַשְׁמַע לָן**, it (the
tanaitic source) lets us hear (that supposition
X is impossible).

L.

קָא מַשְׁמַע לָן
$\left\{\begin{array}{l}\text{וְכִי תֵּימָא ...}\\ \text{לֵימָא ...}\\ \text{מַהוּ דְּתֵימָא ...}\\ \text{נֵימָא ...}\\ \text{קָא סָלְקָא דַּעְתָּךְ ...}\end{array}\right.$

"It might enter your mind" (you might think)

קָא סָלְקָא דַעְתָּךְ
[סָלְקָא דַעְתָּךְ]

A.   Raises a supposition that is later rejected due to the statement made earlier by a Tana or Amora.

L.   קָא סָלְקָא דַעְתָּךְ . . . קָא מַשְׁמַע לָן

Similar: וְכִי תֵימָא, הֲוָה אֲמִינָא, אִם תִּמְצֵי לוֹמַר, אִילֵימָא
סְבָרוּהָ, נֵימָא, מַהוּ דְּתֵימָא, לֵימָא

Related: סָבוּר מִינָּה, אֵימָא

"Question"

קוּשְׁיָא

A.   Introducing a question against an Amora, usually from a tanaitic source.

L.   קוּשְׁיָא . . . קַשְׁיָא

Similar: קַשְׁיָא

Related: תִּיוּבְתָּא, אִיבַּעְיָא לְהוּ

"Read it . . . "

קְרִי . . .

A.   An alternative reading to the biblical verse, other than the way it is written (commonly referred to as כְּתִיב), is suggested. This alternative reading answers the difficulties raised against it.

"It is difficult"

קַשְׁיָא

A.   (1) When positioned within a talmudic discussion, this term indicates a difficulty with an Amora's opinion.
(2) When positioned at the end of a discussion, this term concludes that the

question against the Amora's opinion
remains unresolved.

L. **קַשְׁיָא . . . קַשְׁיָא**

Similar: **קוּשְׁיָא, תְּיוּבְתָּא**

"He learns"   קָתָנֵי
A.   Introduces a tanaitic source.

<u>אוֹת ר</u>

"Rabbi X"   רַב (פְּלוֹנִי)
A.   Title for a Babylonian Amora.

"Rabbi X"   רַבִּי (פְּלוֹנִי)
A.   Title for either a Tana or Amora of the
land of Israel.

"Our Rabbi X"   רַבָּן (פְּלוֹנִי)
A.   Title for the Prince or *Nasi* of the Sanhedrin.

"Our Rabbi X"   רַבָּנָא (פְּלוֹנִי)
A.   Title for the Rabbi of the family of
the Exilarch or *Raish Galuta* in Babylonia.

See **רְמִינְהוּ**   רוּמְיָא

"The merciful one"   רַחֲמָנָא
A.   Although at times this term is simply a

reference to G-d, usually it introduces a
biblical passage.

See רְמִינְהוּ   רָמֵי

"Cast them" (the contradictions) (ו) רְמִינְהוּ
A.   Introducing one source to contradict
another source of equal status (i.e., mishna
against mishna, biblical verse against biblical
verse, etc.). Sometimes the contradiction
arises from two opposing statements of the
same sage.
Same: לְמִירְמָא

אות ש

"It is different"   שָׁאנֵי
A.   This term introduces the distinction
between two seemingly similar cases.

"Something heard" (received teaching) שְׁמוּעָה
A.   A statement of an Amora of Israel as
opposed to a tanaitic statement or statement
from aggada.
Similar: שְׁמַעְתָּא

"Hear from it . . . "   (ש״מ) . . . שְׁמַע מִינָה
A.   (1) When positioned within a
talmudic discussion, this term infers
a conclusion based on the foregoing
discussion.

A.   (2) This term, when positioned at
the end of a talmudic discussion,
emphasizes that the foregoing
supposition or explanation is correct
and conclusive.

L.   שְׁמַע מִינָּהּ . . . שְׁמַע מִינָּהּ

"Something heard" (a received teaching)   שְׁמַעְתָּא

A.   A statement of a Babylonian Amora
as opposed to a tanaitic statement or
statement from aggada.

Similar: שְׁמוּעָה

"He learned"   שָׂנָה

A.   Generally this term indicates a tanaitic teaching.

אוֹת ת

"Come (and) hear."   תָּא שְׁמַע

A.   Introducing a supposition or question
on an Amora, usually brought from a tanaitic
source, occasionally from a biblical verse,
and on rare occasions, from a statement of
an Amora.

"Answer" (refutation)   תִּיוּבְתָּא

A.   Indicating a final refutation against an
Amora's opinion. This refutation is usually
based on a tanaitic source.

L.   תִּיוּבְתָּא (לִפְלוֹנִי) תִּיוּבְתָּא

Related: מֵיתִיבִי, אֵיתִיבֵיהּ

"It is fine"   תֵּינַח

A.   Introduction to a question on an
explanation by demonstrating that
although one aspect is in keeping with
a halacha or logic, another part is not.
The term introduces the part consistent
with the halacha or logic.

L.   תֵּינַח (case A) . . . (case B) . . . מַאי אִיכָּא לְמֵימַר

Similar: הָנִיחָא, בִּשְׁלָמָא

"Let it stand"   תֵּיקוּ

A.   This term concludes that the question
remains unanswered.

"An inference to say"   תַּלְמוּד לוֹמַר (ת״ל)

(Commonly translated:
"It comes to teach us")

A.   Introducing an inference from a
biblical passage as a proof or disproof.

L.   שׁוֹמֵעַ אֲנִי . . . תַּלְמוּד לוֹמַר
        . . . ת״ל . . . יָכוֹל
. . . מִנַּיִן? ת״ל (case B), (case A) אֵין לִי אֶלָּא . . .

"Tana"   תַּנָּא

A.   Reference to a tanaitic sage or an
who memorizes much tanaitic literature.

"Learn"   תְּנָא

A.   Reference to a tanaitic teaching.
Related: תָּנוּ רַבָּנָן, תְּנִי

See תַּנָּא בָּרָא   תַּנָּא דִידָן

"The outside Tana"   תַּנָּא בָּרָא

A.   Reference to a Tana who stated a braita
as opposed to תַּנָּא דִידָן, "Our Tana," who is a
Tana who states a mishna.

"The latter Tana"   תַּנָּא בָּתְרָא

A.   Reference to the last (anonymous)
opinion expressed in a tanaitic source. As
opposed to תַּנָּא קַמָּא, "the first Tana," which
refers to the first Tana of the source. The
תַּנָּא קַמָּא is usually identified with רַבִּי מֵאִיר.

"The first Tana"   (ת״ק) תַּנָּא קַמָּא

A.   See תַּנָּא בָּתְרָא

"It is (like) the tanaitic sages"   תַּנָּאֵי הִיא

A.   The Talmud shows that the present
amoraic dispute rests upon the premise
of an earlier tanaitic dispute.
Same: לֵימָא כְּתַנָּאֵי, כְּתַנָּאֵי

"Our rabbis learned"   (ת״ר) תָּנוּ רַבָּנָן

A.   Introduces an anonymous braita.
The braita is introduced to be discussed
as an independent source, rather than a
support to or question against something.

"Learn" (imperative)   תְּנִי
A.   Introduces an alternative version or
reading of the present version of a tanaitic
source.
Similar: הָכִי קָתָנֵי, הָכִי קָאָמַר

"It was learned"   תַּנְיָא
A.   Introducing a braita or tosefta.

"Another was learned"   תַּנְיָא אִידָךְ
A.   Introducing a second braita or tosefta
that pertains to the immediate discussion.
L.   תָּנֵי חֲדָא . . . וְתַנְיָא אִידָךְ

"I learned"   תְּנֵינָא
A.   An Amora introduces a braita or
tosefta he has learned. (Note that תְּנֵינָא in
the expression תְּנֵינָא לְהָא דְתָנוּ רַבָּנַן has a
completely different application. The
entire phrase should be translated as "I
learned (in a mishna) that which our
rabbis learned (in a braita)."

"We should learn it"   תְּנִיתוּהָ
A.   Opening to a braita, occasionally
a mishna, as an answer to a previously
raised question.

"We learned"   תְּנָן
A.   Introduces a mishna.

"You may conclude"   תִּסְתַּיֵּים
A.   This term introduces a suggestion as
to the identity of the sages in dispute.
When the term begins the sentence,
it is read as a question,"May you
conclude ... ?" When it is repeated a
second time at the end of a sentence,
it is read as a confirming statement,
"You may (in fact) conclude!"
L.   תִּסְתַּיֵּים דַּר׳ פְּלוֹנִי הֲוָה דַּאֲמַר . . . תִּסְתַּיֵּים

"You may solve (the problem)   _____   תִּפְשׁוֹט מ
from _____"
A.   Introduces a source in order
to answer a question raised in the
ongoing discussion. Usually the
answer is later refuted.
L.   תִּפְשׁוֹט מ _____ . . . לְעוֹלָם לָא תִּפְשׁוֹט

"He translated"   תַּרְגֵּם
A.   An Amora explains an unclear tanaitic source.

PART II
RASHI COMMENTARY

RASHI COMMENTARY

Rabbi Shlomo Yitzchaki, better known by the acronym Rashi, is considered the greatest of all biblical and talmudic commentators. Born in Troyes, France, in 1040, Rashi developed what has become the standard commentary to the Talmud. Although he died close to nine centuries ago, his words have taken on a life of their own in the hearts and minds of all those who have studied his interpretations.

The Rashi commentary is an indispensable tool for the study of Talmud. This part is devoted to the understanding of Rashi's method of Talmud commentary. In writing his commentary, Rashi understood his chief role was that of teacher. Pedagogic concerns seem to govern each and every one of his explanations.

Yitzchak Avinari comments, in his introduction to volume two of היכל רש"י, that Rashi had two general concerns. His primary one was "explaining the difficult, incomprehensible, material that, without explanation, cannot be understood at all." The second, and relatively minor concern, was "explaining the material that, by itself, is not difficult, but could possibly be misleading." (Translations are mine.)

At the base of both concerns is the desire to present the Talmud to the reader in a clear and comprehensive manner. Rashi's aim was to make the difficult easy, and the misleading, clear. These are the same concerns a teacher has when presenting material to students. How can difficult material be taught in a clear and understandable way, and how can obstacles be removed that might otherwise mislead or impede the process of understanding? Since Rashi perceived all who studied his works as his students, I have replaced, when appropriate, the word *reader* with the word *student*.

Many books have been written on Rashi's commentary to the Talmud. Some seek to discover general rules Rashi followed in his commentaries, others deal with his use of language, while yet others are concerned with resolving internal contradictions and determining which texts may or may not be attributed to his hand. This work is meant as a reference and guide for the English-speaking student of Talmud in understanding Rashi's commentary.

The purpose of Rashi's commentary is to explain the text. However, many people are unable to utilize Rashi to their fullest advantage. They are not aware of Rashi's objective, or the meaning of the language he uses. This work attempts to address both problems.

Section 1 outlines the various objectives Rashi has in his commentary. I refer to an objective as an "Aspect." Each aspect is highlighted and a brief description follows to further elaborate that aspect. The intention here is to acquaint the student with Rashi's general method of talmudic interpretation. Section 1 is divided into the following areas: Rashi on Mishna, Rashi on Talmud, General Aspects, Aspects of Explaining מִדְרְשֵׁי הֲלָכָה, and Language Aspects. The material in Section 1 has been organized as a brief overview for quick referencing of the different explanatory aspects of Rashi's commentary.

Section 2 is a list of common words and phrases used by Rashi in his commentary. Each word or phrase is translated, with explanatory comments when necessary.

Much of the material in both parts was drawn from דרכו של רשי בפירושו לתלמוד בבלי, by Professor Jonah Fraenkel. Sources and examples have been excluded in order to simplify the use of this reference guide. Those interested in a more scholarly presentation should refer to Professor Jonah Fraenkel's works as well as to other reference works on Rashi's commentary.

Section 1
Aspects of Rashi Commentary

Rashi on Mishna

Background Information

According to Rashi, the only truly accurate explanation of the mishna is the one given by the Talmud. However, when commenting on the mishna, he often does not utilize the Talmud's explanation. Rashi waits, in an attempt to allow the student to discover the Talmud's meaning when it is first disclosed.

Rashi follows the first explanation given in the Talmud

    A when the Talmud initially accepts the first opinion without question, and only later raises objections against it; or

    B when the first of two opinions raised on the mishna best fits the language of the mishna.

The Use of the Expression "מְפֹרָשׁ בַּגְּמָרָא"

Rashi uses the expression מְפֹרָשׁ בַּגְּמָרָא, to indicate any of the following items:

    A There is much discussion in the Talmud on this section of mishna.

    B The Talmud raises a difficulty with this passage of mishna.

    C The Talmud gives the טַעַם for the mishna. (See the aspect טַעַם)

D The Talmud will explain a part of the mishna that seems incomprehensible.

E The Talmud offers an explanation to the mishna that is contrary to the simple reading of the mishna.

Introductions

Rashi makes necessary introductions in the mishna that are meant to simplify the learning of the upcoming talmudic passage.

Review

Rashi will bring in material not necessarily related to the mishna, but that should have been learned, as a review for the student.

Talmudic Explanations

Rashi utilizes the Talmud's explanation of the mishna when it is absolutely required for proper understanding. However, Rashi is as succinct as possible in order to allow the student the opportunity to discover the Talmud's full meaning when the Talmud first discloses it.

The Use of the Expression "טַעַם"

Rashi labors to reveal the טַעַם (reason) for the mishna.

The following is a list of meanings that the word טַעַם
has for Rashi:

A Simple explanations.
B The verse or part of the verse from which the law
   discussed in the Talmud comes. Literary clue:
   טַעְמָא דְ מֵ (פָּסוּק א) (Sage X)
C Central concepts upon which laws are based.
D Explaining the connection or relationship between
   different matters. (Usually one is understood while
   another is not.)

Rashi supplies the טַעַם of the mishna if:
A The Talmud does not.
B The Talmud gives the טַעַם in a discussion not
   directly relating to that particular section of
   mishna.
C The טַעַם is important in understanding other laws
   stated in the mishna.
D The טַעַם is unknown from previous mishna and
   Rashi wants to review it for the student. (See the
   aspect of Review, below.)

Scattered Explanations

When Rashi explains both the mishna and the Talmud, he
often divides his comments between the two places.

Matters Not Discussed by the Talmud

Rashi explains relevant matters of the mishna not discussed in the Talmud.

Rashi on Talmud

General Aspects

The Use of the Expression "טַעַם"

An essential aspect of Rashi on Talmud is to uncover the "טַעַם" (reason) of the Talmud. (See how טַעַם is defined in Aspects of Rashi on Mishna.)

Common literary clues include:

לְיַישֵׁב טְעָמִים, לְיַשֵׁב אֶת הַדָּבָר, וְלָחֵת טַעַם הָגוּן הַטְּעָמִים מְיוּשְׁבִים עַל הַלֵּב

The word טַעְמָא is often not included in Rashi's comments even though he is pursuing the טַעַם of the Talmud. Common literary clues of this kind include:

יָלֵיף לָהּ, יָלְפִינָן לָהּ, _____ מִשׁוּם "(פָּסוּק א)"

Literary clues to indicate that the טַעַם will be explained later in the Talmud include:

מְפָרֵשׁ טַעְמָא לְהַדָּן, מְפָרֵשׁ טַעְמָא לְקַמָּן, טַעְמָא מְפָרֵשׁ בַּתְרָא

Introductions

Rashi offers introductions in order to:

A Simplify the student's learning of the *sugya*

B Encourage independent study. Rashi, on occasion, requires the student to recall his earlier introductory remarks in order to properly understand the present section of Talmud. This requires a student to apply previously acquired knowledge in interpreting new talmudic material.

Talmudic Terminology

The following are the general rules concerning Rashi's explanations of talmudic terms:

A If a term appears twelve or more times throughout the Talmud, Rashi defines it if (1) it is used in an exceptional way, or (2) its normal use in this instance is problematic.

B If a term appears one to five times throughout the Talmud, Rashi defines it on every occasion.

C Between six and eleven times, Rashi defines the term without any specific pattern.

Type of Argumentation

If necessary, Rashi will clarify the type of argumentation used by the Talmud, for example, question/answer/proof/refutation /etc.

Indication to What the Talmud Refers

When a talmudic discussion is unclear, Rashi indicates to what the Talmud's discussion is referring. Common literary clues include:

מְהַדַּר _____ ,קָאֵי, _____ קָא מְהַדַּר, _____ אֲ

Missing Language

Rashi adds key wording to the Talmud text when its meaning is unclear. Often, when doing this, Rashi writes in the style of the Talmud. Unless one is careful, one could mistakenly attribute Rashi's additions to the talmudic text itself.

Early Elicited Explanations

Rashi will introduce information that appears later in the Talmud when without it the present talmudic discussion would remain incomprehensible.

Deferred Explanations

Rashi often indicates that the Talmud will discuss something at a later point in order to alert and to assure the student that the difficulty evoked by the present passage will, in fact, be discussed later. Common literary clues are: כְּדִמְפָרֵשׁ וְאָזֵיל and וּלְקַמָּן מְפָרֵשׁ, כִּדְמְפָרֵשׁ לְקַמָּן

Repeated Explanations

Rashi often repeats explanations in order to
   A refresh a student's memory
   B lend emphasis
   C add an additional point not made earlier (see above aspect)

Rejected Explanations

Occasionally, the Talmud raises an explanation that will later be rejected. When the Talmud fails to alert the student

to the upcoming rejection, Rashi will do so by employing
one of the following literary clues: (קָא סָלְקָא דַעְתָּךְ) קס"ד or
מַשְׁמַע הַשְׁתָּא

Scattered Explanations

Rashi often distributes his comments among different
places. He may explain one point in one place, while a second point in another. Rashi does this so that the student
does not become overloaded with too many ideas all at
once. A complete picture is painted only after taking into
account all of Rashi's comments on a given *sugya.*

Additional Information

Rashi rounds out a Talmud discussion by adding additional
information that is relevant but is not mentioned directly
in the present section of Talmud.

Issues Off the Topic

On occasion, Rashi enters into a side issue (i.e., one that
does not pertain directly to the talmudic discussion). This
may occur for the following reasons:
   A Rashi is attempting to dissuade one from accepting
       an erroneous explanation that was being advanced
       during Rashi's time.
   B Rashi is trying to round out a *sugya* that leaves out
       information that is relevant but not directly related
       to the Talmud's discussion.

C Rashi merely wants to review earlier material to refresh the student's memory (see the aspect of Repeated Explanations).

Conclusion

Rashi often makes summary remarks at the end of a *sugya* that may include the differing viewpoints and halachic reasoning. This is done to make it easier for the student to put things into perspective after a long or complicated *sugya* comes to a conclusion.

Sugya Relationship

Rashi often explains the relationship between two *sugyot* placed next to each other.

Aspects of Explaining מִדְרְשֵׁי הֲלָכָה

Background Information

Rashi distinguishes between "מִדְרָשׁ" and "דְּרָשָׁא" on the one hand and "מַשְׁמָעוּת הַכָּתוּב" (simple meaning of the scriptural text) on the other. דְּרָשָׁא refers to those מִידוֹת שֶׁהַתּוֹרָה נִדְרֶשֶׁת בָּהֶן (whose application is known through מְסוֹרָה). מַשְׁמָעוּת הַכָּתוּב, on the other hand, refers to matters deduced directly from the plain sense of the text and by the מִידָה of קַל וָחוֹמֶר.

Literary clues indicating מַשְׁמָעוּת הַכָּתוּב include:
מַשְׁמָעוּתָא דִקְרָא, מַשְׁמָעוּתָא דְגוּפָא, הַמַשְׁמַע כְּמַשְׁמָעוֹ, מַשְׁמָעוּתָא דְעִנְיָנָא

Relationship Between דְרָשָׁה and פָּסוּק

Generally speaking, Rashi attempts to identify and explain
the relationship between the דְרָשָׁה and the פָּסוּק.

Identification of מִידָה

Rashi often identifies the name of the מִידָה when the Talmud does not do so.

Explanation of מַשְׁמָעוּת הַכָּתוּב

Rashi often explains the מַשְׁמָעוּת הַכָּתוּב when the Talmud
does not discuss the matter.

Language Aspects

The Use of Aramaic

Rashi heavily utilizes the Aramaic of the Talmud in his commentaries.

Word and Phrase Translations

Rashi translates and explains difficult words and phrases.
Some characteristics of Rashi's word translations include

A the use of synonyms

B dual and sometimes triplicate explanations

C one of the explanations using the root of the word being explained

D common everyday examples

The Use of the Word "כְּלוֹמַר"

Rashi uses the word כְּלוֹמַר under the following circumstances:

A When the translation of the words is clear, but the meaning in this instance is not the usual one.

B When the translation is not literal.

C When the text is sufficiently unclear in meaning that, without Rashi's comments, the student may not understand the text properly.

D When the textual version is not exact.

E When explaining sayings or allegorical statements.

F When explaining terms of unusual usage (see the aspect of talmudic terminology).

Talmudic Cases and Examples

Rashi usually gives dual explanations to cases and examples used by the mishna and Talmud.

Variations of Language

Rashi often varies his language slightly in discussing the same matter in different places. The difference in language is seldom meant to change its original interpretation. It is characteristic of Rashi to vary his language.

Word Distinctions

Rashi will distinguish between two similar words in the
Talmud that have different meanings.

Punctuation

On occasion, Rashi suggests punctuation without which
the student's understanding of the text might be incorrect.

Section 2
Common Rashi Words and Phrases

The way of . . .		אוֹרְחָא
The way of the matter (This is the usual way of the matter)	אוֹרְחָא דְמִילְתָא	
The way of the Talmud	אוֹרְחָא דְּתַלְמוּדָא	
He follows [literally: he grasps]		אָחַז
It is needed (to say or learn).		אִיבְּעֵי
It is necessary to learn in the tanaitic source	אִיבָּעֵי לֵיה לְמִתְנֵי	
Which one of them		אֵיזָה מֵהֶן
It appears (refers to)		אַיְירִי
		אִיכָּא
These		אִילֵּן
It was needed		אִיצְטְרִיךְ
There is to him (he maintains)		אִית לֵיה
It follows according to Sage X	Sage X אִית לֵיה לְ	
However		אַךְ
According to Sage X	Sage X אַלִּיבָּא דְ	

We see [infer] (from this)	אַלְמָא
(And) if you were to say …	(וְ) אִם תּוֹמַר … (א״ת)

Rashi raises a question or supposition that is immediately answered or rejected. Usually אִם תּוֹמַר is followed by יֵשׁ לוֹמַר

(And) why	(וְ) אַמַּאי
Even	אַף
Even though	אַף עַל גַּב (אע״ג)
Even though	אַף עַל פִּי (אע״פ)
Even	אֲפִילוּ
(It is) possible	אֶפְשָׁר
We find it	אַשְׁכְּחַן
It is applicable or relevant	
(It refers) on [to] the first part of the matter	אַתְחַלְתָּא דְמִילְתָא
Refutation	אַתְקַפְתָּא
It will be explained (later) in the Talmud. (See the discussion of בִּגְמָרָא מְפָרֵשׁ in the section on aspects)	בִּגְמָרָא מְפָרֵשׁ

(Later) in the Talmud it asks	בַּגְּמָרָא פָּרֵיךְ
Specifically, explicitly	בְּהֶדְיָא
In it (regarding it)	בֵּיהּ

With ease, simply, obvious
    The statement in the
    Talmud should not
    be understood as a question
    or read rhetorically.
	בִּיחוּתָא

Upcoming (in the adjacent discussion)	בְּסָמוּךְ
He asks	בָּעֵי
We need (to say or learn)	בָּעִינַן
It (the matter) is problematic	בַּעְיָא הִיא
Because of	בִּשְׁבִיל

In astonishment
    The Talmudic passage should
    be understood as a question
    and read rhetorically.
	בִּתְמִיהָה

Regarding, in reference to	גַּבֵּי
Itself	גוּפָא
Mistaken, distorted Mistakes, distortions גִּמְגוּמִין	גִּמְגוּם

Rashi uses this word to
describe a long section
of Talmud with
numerous difficulties
on both sides of the
argument (Fraenkel).

(He) learned   גְּמַר

Talmud   גְּמָרָא
Rashi uses this word in
contradistinction to the
Mishna.

(See הָכִי גָּרְסִינָן)   גָּרְסִינָן (גרסי׳)

That there is not   דְּאֵין

Deduction   דּוּקְיָא
Deduction made on close
analytic examination.

That when   דְּלְכִי

Perhaps   דִּלְמָא

Similar, comparable   דָּמֵי

(See עָלְמָא)   דְּעָלְמָא

We deduce [interpret]   דָּרְשִׁינָן
(the verse).

This, but   הָא

This	הַאי
That which	הַאי דְ _____
He/it was	הֲוָה
Since	הוֹאִיל
They are	הֲווּ
It is	הֲוֵי
It is	הֲוָיא
How?	הֵיאַךְ
That is, it is the same as ...	הַיְינוּ ...
(See כָּל הֵיכָא דְקָתָנֵי)	הֵיכָא דְקָתָנֵי
Where?	הֵיכָן
When [where] do we find ....? Where do we find its application or relevancy?	הֵיכָן מָצִינַן . . .?
This Like this we say in *Tractate X* Rashi quotes another talmudic tractate.	הָךְ הָכִי אָמְרִינַן בְּ . . .
Our (textual) version is like this Rashi indicates the correct version of the talmudic text	הָכִי גָּרְסִינַן (ה״ג)

when he knows of other
corrupt textual versions.

Like this it seems (it is heard)   הָכִי מַשְׁמָע

This is its explanation.   הָכִי פֵּירוּשָׁא
    Understand the text or
    statement in the follow-
    ing manner (as opposed
    to any other way).

Like this he/it said   הָכִי קָאָמַר (ה״ק)
    Rashi points out the proper
    way to understand the
    point in question.

These   תְּנֵי

Those   תָּנֵד

Behold   הֲרֵי

Now   הַשְׁתָּא

Now (at this point, or after this   . . . הַשְׁתָּא מַשְׁמָע
point) it appears (that)

(See אִם תּוֹמֵר)   וְאִם תּוֹמֵר

Certainly, definitely   וַדַּאי

And this is the primary (interpretation)   וְזֶה עִיקָר
    Rashi is indicating his preferred
    interpretation (see לִי נִרְאֶה)

And this/that is	וַחֲהוּ
And his colleague, and its counterpart	וְחָבְרוֹ
Is it really so that . . . ? Introducing a question to which a negative answer is expected (Jastrow).	וְכִי . . .
Reason	טַעְמָא
Its reason is explained (later) in the tractate.	טַעְמָא מְפֹרָשׁ בַּגְּמָרָא
Its reason is explained there (in another quoted source)	טַעְמָא מְפֹרָשׁ הָתָם
Its reason is explained further on (in this tractate)	טַעְמָא מְפֹרָשׁ לְקַמָּן
It should be	יְהֵא
He learns (deduces) it	יָלֵיף
There are those that say (it or explain it differently)	יֵשׁ אוֹמְרִין
There is to say, one could say Sometimes Rashi answers a question or rejects a supposition introduced by the words וְאִם תֹּאמַר	יֵשׁ לוֹמַר
There are those that explain (it differently)	יֵשׁ מְפָרְשִׁים

Like the other   כְּאִידָךְ

As if   כְּאִילוּ

For example   כְּגוֹן

As we say (explain) further on   כִּדְאָמְרִינָן לְקַמָּן
(in this tractate)

         As we say (as we explain)   כִּדְאָמְרִינָן בְּ
         in *Tractate X*

As (stated) in the adjacent (discussion)   כִּדְבִסְמוּךְ
         Rashi points out, as a proof
         to his explanation, a passage
         from the nearby Talmud.

In order   כְּדֵי

As it continues (later) to conclude (explain)   כִּדְמְסַיֵּים וְאָזֵיל

As it continues (later) to explain   כִּדְמְפָרֵשׁ וְאָזֵיל

As it explains (later) in this tractate   כִּדְמְפָרֵשׁ בִּגְמָרָא

As it explains further on (in this tractate)   כִּדְמְפָרֵשׁ לְקַמָּן
                                   or
                               כִּדְמְפָרֵשׁ לְקַמֵּיהּ

According to him   כְּוָתֵיהּ

As, like, when (Jastrow)   כִּי

Like this, in this way, in a case, like this (Jastrow)	כִּי הַאי גַּוְונָא
Since	כֵּיוָן
So to, like so/this	כָּךְ
Thus I found (discovered) Usually referring to an expla- nation Rashi learned from a written source as opposed to an oral source (see (כָּךְ שָׁמַעְתִּי, כָּךְ קִבַּלְתִּי	כָּךְ מָצָאתִי
Thus I received (know through tradition) Rashi indicates a teaching he received from one of his teachers (see כָּךְ שָׁמַעְתִּי).	כָּךְ קִבַּלְתִּי
Thus I heard (learned) Rashi indicates a teaching he received from one of his teachers (see כָּךְ קִבַּלְתִּי).	כָּךְ שָׁמַעְתִּי (כ״ש)
Every place (occurrence) that there is ...	כָּל דּוּכְתָּא דְּאִיכָא ...
Every time that it is learned (stated, quoted in a talmudic source)	כָּל הֵיכָא דְּקָתָנֵי ...
That is to say ...	כְּלוֹמַר ...

(See discussion of כְּלוֹמַר in the
section on aspects).

Similar to, like (it is), as (it is)   כְּמוֹ

According to its plain meaning   כְּמַשְׁמָעוֹ

According to its (proper) order   כְּסֵדֶר

It is not explained   לָא אִיפָּרֵשׁ

We do not have (accept) this version   לָא גְּרְסִינָן (ל״ג)
(of the talmudic text)
 Rashi points out that some
 have a mistaken textual version
 of the Talmud. He does not
 want any unsuspecting student
 to be misled by the faulty text.

We do not find (the application of   לָא מָצִינוּ
this case or example)

Not necessarily   לָאו דַּוְקָא
 Rashi points out that the
 Talmud's language in this instance
 is imprecise. No definitive
 halachic conclusions can be
 drawn from the way this
 statement is formulated.

It is of no matter (consequence)   לָאו מִילְתָא הִיא

I did not hear (learn) it   לָה שְׁמַעְתֵּיה (ל״ש)

Therefore	לְהָכִי

It appears to me
    Rashi points out his preferred
    explanation.
    (See וְזֶה עִיקָר).
	לִי נִרְאֶה (ל״נ)

There is not	לֵיכָא

An alternative explanation, or version
    An alternative explan-
    ation or version that
    is preferred
	לִישָׁנָא אַחֲרִינָא (ל״א)

	לִישָׁנָא אַחֲרִינָא וְעִיקָר

A general statement
    Rashi points out with
    this expression that the
    Talmud's language is
    stated generally and
    lacks precise definition
    or meaning.
	לִישָׁנָא בְּעָלְמָא

The expression (version, statement) of the mishna	לִישָׁנָא דְמַתְנִיתִין
(See דִלְכִי)	לְכִי
Therefore	לְכָּךְ
Therefore	לָכֵן
As a support to him (it), to support him (it)	לְסַיּוֹעֵיה

Earlier (in the Talmud it is stated)   לְעֵיל

Because of, according to   לְפִי

Therefore   לְפִיכָךּ

Further on (in this tractate)   לְקַמֵּיה

  Further on (in this tractate)   לְקַמֵּיה בָּעֵי לַהּ
  it (the Talmud) asks a
  question on this (the text
  under discussion).

  Further on (in this   לְקַמֵּיה מְפָרֵשׁ מַאי
  tractate) it (the Talmud)
  explains why (the reason
  or rationale of the text
  under discussion).

Further on (in this tractate)   לְקַמָּן

  Further on (in this   לְקַמָּן יָלֵיף לַהּ
  tractate) it (the Talmud)
  teaches (discusses) about
  it (the text under
  discussion).

  Further on (in this tractate)   לְקַמָּן מְפָרֵשׁ לַהּ
  it (the Talmud) explains it
  (the text under discussion).

  Further on (in this tractate)   לְקַמָּן מְפָרֵשׁ טַעְמָא
  it (the Talmud) explains the
  reason (or rationale for the
  text under discussion).

  Further on (in this   לְקַמָּן מְפָרֵשׁ מַאי קָאָמַר
  tractate) it (the Talmud)
  explains what was said
  (the reason or rationale

behind what was said in the text under discussion). Further on (in this tractate) it (the Talmud) asks (a question on the text under discussion).	לְקַמָּן פְּרִיךְ . . .

An expression (statement) of	לָשׁוֹן . . .
An expression of question	לְשׁוֹן בַּעְיָא
The Talmud's expression (language) (See לִישָׁנָא בְּעָלְמָא)	לְשׁוֹן הַתַּלְמוּד
My teacher's expression (explanation, version, language)	לְשׁוֹן מוֹרִי
An expression of one who is questioning	לְשׁוֹן מַקְשֶׁה
An expression of question	לְשׁוֹן קוּשְׁיָא
The _____ expression (explanation, version, language) I heard (learned or was taught)	לְשׁוֹן _____ שָׁמַעְתִּי
An expression of question	לְשׁוֹן שְׁאֵלָה
An expression of astonishment (this expression of the Talmud should be understood rhetorically; see בִּתְמִיהָה)	לְשׁוֹן תֵּימָה
An expression of an answer to a question	לְשׁוֹן תְּשׁוּבַת שְׁאֵלָה

It returns (refers to)	מְהַדַּר
On the _____, it (the matter under discussion) refers.	אַ _____ מְהַדַּר
It (the matter under	מְהַדַּר לְעֵיל

discussion) refers to
an earlier (section)
    Rashi specifies to
    what the words of
    the Talmud are
    referring (see קָאֵי).

Establishes [applies] (the   מוֹקִי
law or case)
    We establish   מוֹקִים

We establish (conclude, decide)   מָקְמִינַן

Something   מִידֵי

It appears   מַיְירֵי

Matter, word   מִילְתָא
    See under separate   אַתְחַלְתָא דְמִילְתָא
    entry
    The matter was   מִילְתָא בְּאַפֵּי נַפְשֵׁיה קָאֲמַר
    said by itself (as an
    isolated or inde-
    pendent instance
    from other matters).
    A matter of astonish-   מִילְתָא דִתְמִיהָה
    ment (See בִּתְמִיהָה
    and לְשׁוֹן תֵּימַה)
    The explanation   פֵּירוּשָׁא דְמִילְתָא
    of the matter

Who finds (cases or examples of this)   מִי מָצֵי

Nevertheless	מִכָּל מָקוֹם (מ״מ)
It follows A deduction is being made.	מִכְּלַל
(See מַשְׁמָע)	מִמַּשְׁמָע

Conclusion
    End of the matter
    End of the question
        Conclusion of a
        discussion, not to be
        confused with the
        final decision. מַסְקָנָא
        is the opposite
        of אַתְחַלְתָּא דְמִילְתָא.
	מַסְקָנָא
	מַסְקָנָא דְמִילְתָא
	מַסְקָנָא דְקוּשְׁיָא

It makes sense (it is apparent)	מִסְתַּבְּרָא
From the mouth of (directly from) my teacher	מִפִּי מוֹרִי
Because	מִפְּנֵי

Explained in the Talmud
    See the discussion of
    מְפֹרָשׁ בַּגְּמָרָא in the
    section on aspects.
	מְפֹרָשׁ בַּגְּמָרָא

It is applicable [literally: it is found to establish it]	מָצֵי לְאוֹקְמֵי

Because of ...	מִשׁוּם . . .
It is found (it has application)	מִשְׁכַּחַתְּ לָהּ
It indicates (we infer from the foregoing that ...)	מַשְׁמַע
Now (at this point) it (appears to) infers	מַשְׁמָע הַשְׁתָּא

    Rashi provides an explanation
    for the student that the Talmud
    offers, then rejects in favor
    of a preferred explanation.

Its (plain) meaning	מַשְׁמָעוּת
	מַשְׁמָעוּת הַכָּתוּב

    See the discussion
    of מַשְׁמָעוּת הַכָּתוּב in the
    section on aspects.

It answers	מְשַׁנֵּי (וּ)
We answer	מְשַׁנִּינַן
Because of this	מִתּוֹךְ כָּךְ
They are	נִינְהוּ
Also	נַמֵּי
It ends up [literally: it is found]	נִמְצָא
He holds (learns)	נָקַט

It appears (it seems to mean . . .)   נִרְאֶה

Sugya (topical discussion in   סוּגְיָא
the Talmud)
   The *sugya* that we are   סוּגְיָא דִּשְׁמַעְתִּין
   hearing (learning)
     This word is used
     as a general descrip-
     tion for the given
     talmudic discussion.

Conclusion (See מַסְקָנָא)   סִיוּמָא
   Conclusion of the matter   סִיוּמָא דְּמִילְתָא
   Conclusion of the   סִיוּמָא דְּפִירְכָא
   question

Its (proper) order   סִידְרָא
   The (proper) order of   סִידְרָא דְּמַתְנִיתִין
   the mishna (i.e. the
   cases or parts of the
   mishna)

Support   סַיְיעְתָּא

Until now   עַד הַשְׁתָּא

Primary, fundamental, essential   עִיקָר
   See under separate entry   וְזֶה עִיקָר
   The primary (explana-   עִיקָר בְּעֵינַי . . .
   tion) according to me is . . .
   And the first (explanation)   וְרִאשׁוֹן עִיקָר
   is the primary one

Certainly [literally: you are forced (to say)]	עַל כָּרְחָךְ (ע״כ)
On condition On this condition	עַל מְנָת עַל מְנָת כֵּן

(The) world
    The word refers not to the
    world in the general but
    to the specific world of the
    commentators on the given
    talmudic passage.
	עָלְמָא

Another interpretation	פֵּירוּשׁ אַחֵר
It is a question	פִּירְכָא הִיא
Ask We ask	פָּרִיךְ פָּרְכִינָן
Simple (obvious) meaning	פְּשִׁיטָה

It lets us hear
    We infer from the
    foregoing that …
	קָא מַשְׁמַע לָן (קמ״ל)

It would enter one's
mind (to think) …
    Rashi provides an
    explanation that the
    Talmud offers, then
    rejects in favor of a
    preferred explanation.
	קָא סָלְקָא דַעְתֵּיהּ (קס״ד)

Refers to	קָאֵי
On _____ it refers	אַ _____ קָאֵי
Rashi specifies the words to which the Talmud refers (See מְהַדַּר)	

It is a question	קוּשְׁיָא הִיא
It is called	קָרוּי
Difficulty, question	קַשְׁיָא
It is learned (in a tanaitic source)	קָתָנֵי
My Rabbis (teachers) explained	רַבּוֹתַי פֵּרְשׁוּ
(The) running (give and take of the talmudic passage) Rashi uses this word to describe the give and take of the Talmud's discussion.	רִיהַטָא
That it is not, that one does not	שֶׁאֵינוֹ
Any	שׁוּם
General approach, view, opinion, position	שִׁיטָה
Answer	שִׁינוּיָא
Learning, teaching, section of Talmud	שְׁמַעְתָּא, שְׁמַעְתָּתָא

I heard (learned from a teacher)   שְׁמַעְתִּי

Our section of Talmud   שְׁמַעְתִּין

(See שִׁנוּיָה)   שְׁנוּיָה

We learned   שָׁנִינוּ

Permissible   שָׁרֵי

Let it be   תִּהְא

Refutation   תְּיוּבְתָּא

Talmud   תַּלְמוּד

Talmud, oral tradition or teaching   תַּלְמוּדָא

Follow the _____ expression   _____ תְּפוֹס לְשׁוֹן
(interpretation, see עִיקָר)

Explain, explanation, answer   תָּרֵץ, תָּרְצְתָא, תָּרִיצוּתָא

About the Author

Rabbi Scot A. Berman was born in Alma, Michigan, and received his rabbinic ordination from the Hebrew Theological College in Skokie, Illinois, in 1908. He holds a masters degree in curriculum and instruction from Loyola University in Chicago. Rabbi Berman developed many of his ideas about teaching Talmud while head of the Talmud department, and later as assistant principal of, Ida Crown Jewish Academy. From 1992-1994, Rabbi Berman studied in Jerusalem as a Jerusalem Fellow. He was principal of Rabbi David L. Silver Yeshiva Academy in Harrisburg, Pennsylvania, and is currently principal of the Joseph Kushner Hebrew Academy High School in Livingston, New Jersey. Rabbi Berman lives in West Orange, New Jersey, with his wife and four children.